Address Book

This book belongs to

_____

_____

A

Name:
Address:
Mobile:
Work:
Home:
Fax:
Email:
Birthday:
Notes:

Name:
Address:
Mobile:
Work:
Home:
Fax:
Email:
Birthday:
Notes:

A

Name:
Address:
Mobile:
Work:
Home:
Fax:
Email:
Birthday:
Notes:

Name:
Address:
Mobile:
Work:
Home:
Fax:
Email:
Birthday:
Notes:

A

Name:
Address:
Mobile:
Work:
Home:
Fax:
Email:
Birthday:
Notes:

Name:
Address:
Mobile:
Work:
Home:
Fax:
Email:
Birthday:
Notes:

A

Name:

Address:

Mobile:

Work:

Home:

Fax:

Email:

Birthday:

Notes:

Name:

Address:

Mobile:

Work:

Home:

Fax:

Email:

Birthday:

Notes:

B

Name:
Address:
Mobile:
Work:
Home:
Fax:
Email:
Birthday:
Notes:

Name:
Address:
Mobile:
Work:
Home:
Fax:
Email:
Birthday:
Notes:

B

Name:

Address:

Mobile:

Work:

Home:

Fax:

Email:

Birthday:

Notes:

Name:

Address:

Mobile:

Work:

Home:

Fax:

Email:

Birthday:

Notes:

B

Name:

Address:

Mobile:

Work:

Home:

Fax:

Email:

Birthday:

Notes:

Name:

Address:

Mobile:

Work:

Home:

Fax:

Email:

Birthday:

Notes:

B

Name:

Address:

Mobile:

Work:

Home:

Fax:

Email:

Birthday:

Notes:

Name:

Address:

Mobile:

Work:

Home:

Fax:

Email:

Birthday:

Notes:

C

Name:
Address:
Mobile:
Work:
Home:
Fax:
Email:
Birthday:
Notes:

Name:
Address:
Mobile:
Work:
Home:
Fax:
Email:
Birthday:
Notes:

C

Name:
Address:
Mobile:
Work:
Home:
Fax:
Email:
Birthday:
Notes:

Name:
Address:
Mobile:
Work:
Home:
Fax:
Email:
Birthday:
Notes:

C

Name: _____
Address: _____
Mobile: _____
Work: _____
Home: _____
Fax: _____
Email: _____
Birthday: _____
Notes: _____
_____
_____

Name: _____
Address: _____
Mobile: _____
Work: _____
Home: _____
Fax: _____
Email: _____
Birthday: _____
Notes: _____
_____
_____

C

Name:

Address:

Mobile:

Work:

Home:

Fax:

Email:

Birthday:

Notes:

Name:

Address:

Mobile:

Work:

Home:

Fax:

Email:

Birthday:

Notes:

D

Name:
Address:
Mobile:
Work:
Home:
Fax:
Email:
Birthday:
Notes:

Name:
Address:
Mobile:
Work:
Home:
Fax:
Email:
Birthday:
Notes:

D

Name:

Address:

Mobile:

Work:

Home:

Fax:

Email:

Birthday:

Notes:

Name:

Address:

Mobile:

Work:

Home:

Fax:

Email:

Birthday:

Notes:

D

Name:
Address:
Mobile:
Work:
Home:
Fax:
Email:
Birthday:
Notes:

Name:
Address:
Mobile:
Work:
Home:
Fax:
Email:
Birthday:
Notes:

Name:

Address:

Mobile:

Work:

Home:

Fax:

Email:

Birthday:

Notes:

Name:

Address:

Mobile:

Work:

Home:

Fax:

Email:

Birthday:

Notes:

E

Name:

Address:

Mobile:

Work:

Home:

Fax:

Email:

Birthday:

Notes:

Name:

Address:

Mobile:

Work:

Home:

Fax:

Email:

Birthday:

Notes:

E

Name:

Address:

Mobile:

Work:

Home:

Fax:

Email:

Birthday:

Notes:

Name:

Address:

Mobile:

Work:

Home:

Fax:

Email:

Birthday:

Notes:

E

Name:
Address:
Mobile:
Work:
Home:
Fax:
Email:
Birthday:
Notes:

Name:
Address:
Mobile:
Work:
Home:
Fax:
Email:
Birthday:
Notes:

E

Name:

Address:

Mobile:

Work:

Home:

Fax:

Email:

Birthday:

Notes:

Name:

Address:

Mobile:

Work:

Home:

Fax:

Email:

Birthday:

Notes:

F

Name:

Address:

Mobile:

Work:

Home:

Fax:

Email:

Birthday:

Notes:

Name:

Address:

Mobile:

Work:

Home:

Fax:

Email:

Birthday:

Notes:

F

Name:

Address:

Mobile:

Work:

Home:

Fax:

Email:

Birthday:

Notes:

Name:

Address:

Mobile:

Work:

Home:

Fax:

Email:

Birthday:

Notes:

F

Name:
Address:
Mobile:
Work:
Home:
Fax:
Email:
Birthday:
Notes:

Name:
Address:
Mobile:
Work:
Home:
Fax:
Email:
Birthday:
Notes:

F

Name:

Address:

Mobile:

Work:

Home:

Fax:

Email:

Birthday:

Notes:

Name:

Address:

Mobile:

Work:

Home:

Fax:

Email:

Birthday:

Notes:

G

Name:

Address:

Mobile:

Work:

Home:

Fax:

Email:

Birthday:

Notes:

Name:

Address:

Mobile:

Work:

Home:

Fax:

Email:

Birthday:

Notes:

G

Name:

Address:

Mobile:

Work:

Home:

Fax:

Email:

Birthday:

Notes:

Name:

Address:

Mobile:

Work:

Home:

Fax:

Email:

Birthday:

Notes:

G

Name:

Address:

Mobile:

Work:

Home:

Fax:

Email:

Birthday:

Notes:

Name:

Address:

Mobile:

Work:

Home:

Fax:

Email:

Birthday:

Notes:

G

Name:

Address:

Mobile:

Work:

Home:

Fax:

Email:

Birthday:

Notes:

Name:

Address:

Mobile:

Work:

Home:

Fax:

Email:

Birthday:

Notes:

H

Name:
Address:
Mobile:
Work:
Home:
Fax:
Email:
Birthday:
Notes:

Name:
Address:
Mobile:
Work:
Home:
Fax:
Email:
Birthday:
Notes:

Name:

Address:

Mobile:

Work:

Home:

Fax:

Email:

Birthday:

Notes:

Name:

Address:

Mobile:

Work:

Home:

Fax:

Email:

Birthday:

Notes:

H

Name:

Address:

Mobile:

Work:

Home:

Fax:

Email:

Birthday:

Notes:

Name:

Address:

Mobile:

Work:

Home:

Fax:

Email:

Birthday:

Notes:

Name:
Address:
Mobile:
Work:
Home:
Fax:
Email:
Birthday:
Notes:

Name:
Address:
Mobile:
Work:
Home:
Fax:
Email:
Birthday:
Notes:

Name:

Address:

Mobile:

Work:

Home:

Fax:

Email:

Birthday:

Notes:

Name:

Address:

Mobile:

Work:

Home:

Fax:

Email:

Birthday:

Notes:

I

Name:
Address:
Mobile:
Work:
Home:
Fax:
Email:
Birthday:
Notes:

Name:
Address:
Mobile:
Work:
Home:
Fax:
Email:
Birthday:
Notes:

I

Name:
Address:
Mobile:
Work:
Home:
Fax:
Email:
Birthday:
Notes:

Name:
Address:
Mobile:
Work:
Home:
Fax:
Email:
Birthday:
Notes:

I

Name:

Address:

Mobile:

Work:

Home:

Fax:

Email:

Birthday:

Notes:

Name:

Address:

Mobile:

Work:

Home:

Fax:

Email:

Birthday:

Notes:

J

Name:

Address:

Mobile:

Work:

Home:

Fax:

Email:

Birthday:

Notes:

Name:

Address:

Mobile:

Work:

Home:

Fax:

Email:

Birthday:

Notes:

J

Name:

Address:

Mobile:

Work:

Home:

Fax:

Email:

Birthday:

Notes:

Name:

Address:

Mobile:

Work:

Home:

Fax:

Email:

Birthday:

Notes:

J

Name:

Address:

Mobile:

Work:

Home:

Fax:

Email:

Birthday:

Notes:

Name:

Address:

Mobile:

Work:

Home:

Fax:

Email:

Birthday:

Notes:

J

Name:

Address:

Mobile:

Work:

Home:

Fax:

Email:

Birthday:

Notes:

Name:

Address:

Mobile:

Work:

Home:

Fax:

Email:

Birthday:

Notes:

K

Name:

Address:

Mobile:

Work:

Home:

Fax:

Email:

Birthday:

Notes:

Name:

Address:

Mobile:

Work:

Home:

Fax:

Email:

Birthday:

Notes:

Name:
Address:
Mobile:
Work:
Home:
Fax:
Email:
Birthday:
Notes:

Name:
Address:
Mobile:
Work:
Home:
Fax:
Email:
Birthday:
Notes:

K

Name:
Address:
Mobile:
Work:
Home:
Fax:
Email:
Birthday:
Notes:

Name:
Address:
Mobile:
Work:
Home:
Fax:
Email:
Birthday:
Notes:

Name:

Address:

Mobile:

Work:

Home:

Fax:

Email:

Birthday:

Notes:

Name:

Address:

Mobile:

Work:

Home:

Fax:

Email:

Birthday:

Notes:

L

Name:

Address:

Mobile:

Work:

Home:

Fax:

Email:

Birthday:

Notes:

Name:

Address:

Mobile:

Work:

Home:

Fax:

Email:

Birthday:

Notes:

L

Name:

Address:

Mobile:

Work:

Home:

Fax:

Email:

Birthday:

Notes:

Name:

Address:

Mobile:

Work:

Home:

Fax:

Email:

Birthday:

Notes:

L

Name:

Address:

Mobile:

Work:

Home:

Fax:

Email:

Birthday:

Notes:

Name:

Address:

Mobile:

Work:

Home:

Fax:

Email:

Birthday:

Notes:

L

Name:
Address:
Mobile:
Work:
Home:
Fax:
Email:
Birthday:
Notes:

Name:
Address:
Mobile:
Work:
Home:
Fax:
Email:
Birthday:
Notes:

M

Name:

Address:

Mobile:

Work:

Home:

Fax:

Email:

Birthday:

Notes:

Name:

Address:

Mobile:

Work:

Home:

Fax:

Email:

Birthday:

Notes:

M

Name:
Address:
Mobile:
Work:
Home:
Fax:
Email:
Birthday:
Notes:

Name:
Address:
Mobile:
Work:
Home:
Fax:
Email:
Birthday:
Notes:

M

Name:
Address:
Mobile:
Work:
Home:
Fax:
Email:
Birthday:
Notes:

Name:
Address:
Mobile:
Work:
Home:
Fax:
Email:
Birthday:
Notes:

M

Name:
Address:
Mobile:
Work:
Home:
Fax:
Email:
Birthday:
Notes:

Name:
Address:
Mobile:
Work:
Home:
Fax:
Email:
Birthday:
Notes:

N

Name:
Address:
Mobile:
Work:
Home:
Fax:
Email:
Birthday:
Notes:

Name:
Address:
Mobile:
Work:
Home:
Fax:
Email:
Birthday:
Notes:

N

Name:

Address:

Mobile:

Work:

Home:

Fax:

Email:

Birthday:

Notes:

Name:

Address:

Mobile:

Work:

Home:

Fax:

Email:

Birthday:

Notes:

N

Name:
Address:
Mobile:
Work:
Home:
Fax:
Email:
Birthday:
Notes:

Name:
Address:
Mobile:
Work:
Home:
Fax:
Email:
Birthday:
Notes:

N

Name:
Address:
Mobile:
Work:
Home:
Fax:
Email:
Birthday:
Notes:

Name:
Address:
Mobile:
Work:
Home:
Fax:
Email:
Birthday:
Notes:

O

Name:

Address:

Mobile:

Work:

Home:

Fax:

Email:

Birthday:

Notes:

Name:

Address:

Mobile:

Work:

Home:

Fax:

Email:

Birthday:

Notes:

Name:

Address:

Mobile:

Work:

Home:

Fax:

Email:

Birthday:

Notes:

Name:

Address:

Mobile:

Work:

Home:

Fax:

Email:

Birthday:

Notes:

O

Name:

Address:

Mobile:

Work:

Home:

Fax:

Email:

Birthday:

Notes:

Name:

Address:

Mobile:

Work:

Home:

Fax:

Email:

Birthday:

Notes:

Name:
Address:
Mobile:
Work:
Home:
Fax:
Email:
Birthday:
Notes:

Name:
Address:
Mobile:
Work:
Home:
Fax:
Email:
Birthday:
Notes:

P

Name:

Address:

Mobile:

Work:

Home:

Fax:

Email:

Birthday:

Notes:

Name:

Address:

Mobile:

Work:

Home:

Fax:

Email:

Birthday:

Notes:

P

Name:

Address:

Mobile:

Work:

Home:

Fax:

Email:

Birthday:

Notes:

Name:

Address:

Mobile:

Work:

Home:

Fax:

Email:

Birthday:

Notes:

P

Name:
Address:
Mobile:
Work:
Home:
Fax:
Email:
Birthday:
Notes:

Name:
Address:
Mobile:
Work:
Home:
Fax:
Email:
Birthday:
Notes:

P

Name:

Address:

Mobile:

Work:

Home:

Fax:

Email:

Birthday:

Notes:

Name:

Address:

Mobile:

Work:

Home:

Fax:

Email:

Birthday:

Notes:

Name:
Address:
Mobile:
Work:
Home:
Fax:
Email:
Birthday:
Notes:

Name:
Address:
Mobile:
Work:
Home:
Fax:
Email:
Birthday:
Notes:

Q

Name:

Address:

Mobile:

Work:

Home:

Fax:

Email:

Birthday:

Notes:

Name:

Address:

Mobile:

Work:

Home:

Fax:

Email:

Birthday:

Notes:

Name:
Address:
Mobile:
Work:
Home:
Fax:
Email:
Birthday:
Notes:

Name:
Address:
Mobile:
Work:
Home:
Fax:
Email:
Birthday:
Notes:

Name:

Address:

Mobile:

Work:

Home:

Fax:

Email:

Birthday:

Notes:

Name:

Address:

Mobile:

Work:

Home:

Fax:

Email:

Birthday:

Notes:

R

Name:
Address:
Mobile:
Work:
Home:
Fax:
Email:
Birthday:
Notes:

Name:
Address:
Mobile:
Work:
Home:
Fax:
Email:
Birthday:
Notes:

R

Name:

Address:

Mobile:

Work:

Home:

Fax:

Email:

Birthday:

Notes:

Name:

Address:

Mobile:

Work:

Home:

Fax:

Email:

Birthday:

Notes:

R

Name:
Address:
Mobile:
Work:
Home:
Fax:
Email:
Birthday:
Notes:

Name:
Address:
Mobile:
Work:
Home:
Fax:
Email:
Birthday:
Notes:

R

Name:
Address:
Mobile:
Work:
Home:
Fax:
Email:
Birthday:
Notes:

Name:
Address:
Mobile:
Work:
Home:
Fax:
Email:
Birthday:
Notes:

S

Name:
Address:
Mobile:
Work:
Home:
Fax:
Email:
Birthday:
Notes:

Name:
Address:
Mobile:
Work:
Home:
Fax:
Email:
Birthday:
Notes:

S

Name:

Address:

Mobile:

Work:

Home:

Fax:

Email:

Birthday:

Notes:

Name:

Address:

Mobile:

Work:

Home:

Fax:

Email:

Birthday:

Notes:

S

Name:
Address:
Mobile:
Work:
Home:
Fax:
Email:
Birthday:
Notes:

Name:
Address:
Mobile:
Work:
Home:
Fax:
Email:
Birthday:
Notes:

S

Name:

Address:

Mobile:

Work:

Home:

Fax:

Email:

Birthday:

Notes:

Name:

Address:

Mobile:

Work:

Home:

Fax:

Email:

Birthday:

Notes:

T

Name:

Address:

Mobile:

Work:

Home:

Fax:

Email:

Birthday:

Notes:

Name:

Address:

Mobile:

Work:

Home:

Fax:

Email:

Birthday:

Notes:

T

Name:

Address:

Mobile:

Work:

Home:

Fax:

Email:

Birthday:

Notes:

Name:

Address:

Mobile:

Work:

Home:

Fax:

Email:

Birthday:

Notes:

T

Name:
Address:
Mobile:
Work:
Home:
Fax:
Email:
Birthday:
Notes:

Name:
Address:
Mobile:
Work:
Home:
Fax:
Email:
Birthday:
Notes:

T

Name:

Address:

Mobile:

Work:

Home:

Fax:

Email:

Birthday:

Notes:

Name:

Address:

Mobile:

Work:

Home:

Fax:

Email:

Birthday:

Notes:

U

Name:
Address:
Mobile:
Work:
Home:
Fax:
Email:
Birthday:
Notes:

Name:
Address:
Mobile:
Work:
Home:
Fax:
Email:
Birthday:
Notes:

Name:

Address:

Mobile:

Work:

Home:

Fax:

Email:

Birthday:

Notes:

Name:

Address:

Mobile:

Work:

Home:

Fax:

Email:

Birthday:

Notes:

U

Name:
Address:
Mobile:
Work:
Home:
Fax:
Email:
Birthday:
Notes:

Name:
Address:
Mobile:
Work:
Home:
Fax:
Email:
Birthday:
Notes:

U

Name:

Address:

Mobile:

Work:

Home:

Fax:

Email:

Birthday:

Notes:

Name:

Address:

Mobile:

Work:

Home:

Fax:

Email:

Birthday:

Notes:

V

Name:
Address:
Mobile:
Work:
Home:
Fax:
Email:
Birthday:
Notes:

Name:
Address:
Mobile:
Work:
Home:
Fax:
Email:
Birthday:
Notes:

Name:

Address:

Mobile:

Work:

Home:

Fax:

Email:

Birthday:

Notes:

Name:

Address:

Mobile:

Work:

Home:

Fax:

Email:

Birthday:

Notes:

V

Name:
Address:
Mobile:
Work:
Home:
Fax:
Email:
Birthday:
Notes:

Name:
Address:
Mobile:
Work:
Home:
Fax:
Email:
Birthday:
Notes:

Name:

Address:

Mobile:

Work:

Home:

Fax:

Email:

Birthday:

Notes:

Name:

Address:

Mobile:

Work:

Home:

Fax:

Email:

Birthday:

Notes:

Name:
Address:
Mobile:
Work:
Home:
Fax:
Email:
Birthday:
Notes:

Name:
Address:
Mobile:
Work:
Home:
Fax:
Email:
Birthday:
Notes:

Name:

Address:

Mobile:

Work:

Home:

Fax:

Email:

Birthday:

Notes:

Name:

Address:

Mobile:

Work:

Home:

Fax:

Email:

Birthday:

Notes:

Name: _____
Address: _____
Mobile: _____
Work: _____
Home: _____
Fax: _____
Email: _____
Birthday: _____
Notes: _____
_____
_____

Name: _____
Address: _____
Mobile: _____
Work: _____
Home: _____
Fax: _____
Email: _____
Birthday: _____
Notes: _____
_____
_____

Name:
Address:
Mobile:
Work:
Home:
Fax:
Email:
Birthday:
Notes:

Name:
Address:
Mobile:
Work:
Home:
Fax:
Email:
Birthday:
Notes:

X

Name:
Address:
Mobile:
Work:
Home:
Fax:
Email:
Birthday:
Notes:

Name:
Address:
Mobile:
Work:
Home:
Fax:
Email:
Birthday:
Notes:

X

Name:

Address:

Mobile:

Work:

Home:

Fax:

Email:

Birthday:

Notes:

Name:

Address:

Mobile:

Work:

Home:

Fax:

Email:

Birthday:

Notes:

Name:
Address:
Mobile:
Work:
Home:
Fax:
Email:
Birthday:
Notes:

Name:
Address:
Mobile:
Work:
Home:
Fax:
Email:
Birthday:
Notes:

X

Name:

Address:

Mobile:

Work:

Home:

Fax:

Email:

Birthday:

Notes:

Name:

Address:

Mobile:

Work:

Home:

Fax:

Email:

Birthday:

Notes:

Y

Name:

Address:

Mobile:

Work:

Home:

Fax:

Email:

Birthday:

Notes:

Name:

Address:

Mobile:

Work:

Home:

Fax:

Email:

Birthday:

Notes:

Y

Name:

Address:

Mobile:

Work:

Home:

Fax:

Email:

Birthday:

Notes:

Name:

Address:

Mobile:

Work:

Home:

Fax:

Email:

Birthday:

Notes:

Y

Name:
Address:
Mobile:
Work:
Home:
Fax:
Email:
Birthday:
Notes:

Name:
Address:
Mobile:
Work:
Home:
Fax:
Email:
Birthday:
Notes:

Y

Name:
Address:
Mobile:
Work:
Home:
Fax:
Email:
Birthday:
Notes:

Name:
Address:
Mobile:
Work:
Home:
Fax:
Email:
Birthday:
Notes:

Z

Name:

Address:

Mobile:

Work:

Home:

Fax:

Email:

Birthday:

Notes:

Name:

Address:

Mobile:

Work:

Home:

Fax:

Email:

Birthday:

Notes:

Z

Name:
Address:
Mobile:
Work:
Home:
Fax:
Email:
Birthday:
Notes:

Name:
Address:
Mobile:
Work:
Home:
Fax:
Email:
Birthday:
Notes:

Z

Name:

Address:

Mobile:

Work:

Home:

Fax:

Email:

Birthday:

Notes:

Name:

Address:

Mobile:

Work:

Home:

Fax:

Email:

Birthday:

Notes:

Z

Name:

Address:

Mobile:

Work:

Home:

Fax:

Email:

Birthday:

Notes:

Name:

Address:

Mobile:

Work:

Home:

Fax:

Email:

Birthday:

Notes:

AB

Name:
Address:
Mobile:
Work:
Home:
Fax:
Email:
Birthday:
Notes:

Name:
Address:
Mobile:
Work:
Home:
Fax:
Email:
Birthday:
Notes:

AB

Name:

Address:

Mobile:

Work:

Home:

Fax:

Email:

Birthday:

Notes:

Name:

Address:

Mobile:

Work:

Home:

Fax:

Email:

Birthday:

Notes:

AB

Name:
Address:
Mobile:
Work:
Home:
Fax:
Email:
Birthday:
Notes:

Name:
Address:
Mobile:
Work:
Home:
Fax:
Email:
Birthday:
Notes:

AB

Name:

Address:

Mobile:

Work:

Home:

Fax:

Email:

Birthday:

Notes:

Name:

Address:

Mobile:

Work:

Home:

Fax:

Email:

Birthday:

Notes:

AC

Name:
Address:
Mobile:
Work:
Home:
Fax:
Email:
Birthday:
Notes:

Name:
Address:
Mobile:
Work:
Home:
Fax:
Email:
Birthday:
Notes:

Made in the USA
Middletown, DE
09 January 2025